TOP CLASS

Punctuation

Year 3

Hopscotch
A division of MA Education Ltd

John Murray

Published by Hopscotch, a division of MA Education, St Jude's Church, Dulwich Road, London, SE24 0PB
www.hopscotchbooks.com
020 7738 5454

©2014 MA Education Ltd

Written by John Murray

Series designed by Claire White, Fonthill Creative, 01722 717029

Illustrations by Emma Turner and Sara Cullen

Associate Publisher: Angela Morano Shaw

ISBN 9781909860179

All rights reserved. This resource is sold subject to the condition that it shall not, by way of trade or otherwise, be lent, hired out or otherwise circulated without the publisher's prior consent in any form of binding or cover other than that in which it is published and without a similar condition, including this condition, being imposed upon the subsequent purchaser.

No part of this publication may be reproduced, stored in a retrieval system, or transmitted, in any form or by any means, electronic, mechanical, photocopying, recording or otherwise, without the prior permission of the publisher, except where photocopying for educational purposes within the school or other educational establishment that has purchased this book is expressly permitted in the text.

Every effort has been made to trace the owners of copyright of material in this book and the publisher apologises for any inadvertent omissions. Any persons claiming copyright for any material should contact the publisher who will be happy to pay the permission fees agreed between them and who will amend the information in this book on any subsequent reprint.

Contents Page

Introduction — 6

Capital Letters — 8

Full Stops — 12

Question Marks — 16

Exclamation Marks — 20

Commas I (within lists) — 24

Commas II (within clauses) — 28

Inverted Commas — 32

Apostrophes (for omission) — 36

Apostrophes (for possession) — 40

Brackets — 44

Ellipses — 48

Colons — 52

Semi-colons — 56

Punctuation for Parenthesis — 60

Introduction

Top Class is a series that endeavours to combine traditional approaches to the teaching and learning of grammar, punctuation and vocabulary with new techniques and activities that support and encourage good learning.

The three core areas have been separated into three distinct books aimed primarily at Key Stage 2. The three books ought to be used in conjunction with each other in order to provide learners with a wider learning environment and for them to understand that these core elements of Literacy work together and are not to be applied in isolation.

Specific elements of the new Key Stage 3 National Curriculum have also been included in order to introduce Key Stage 2 learners to more complex grammatical constructions and vocabulary as they make their transition from attaining Level 4 to Level 5 in writing.

Each book, one for each Year group in Key Stage 2, aims to promote discussion about specific areas of Literacy and provide experiences and opportunities to use and apply what they have learnt.

The three books are as follows:

- **Top Class – Grammar**
- **Top Class – Punctuation**
- **Top Class – Vocabulary**

Each book contains lessons that develop a 'top-down' approach, allowing learners to see how we use language in context, not simply *when* we use a particular word, punctuation mark or grammatical construct but *how* to use it to its best effect when writing independently.

As such, it actively promotes the core principle that to learn grammar and punctuation well and to extend your personal vocabulary effectively, then you must not only see these particular elements of Literacy within authentic and meaningful context and settings but you must then have the opportunity to apply what you have understood in your own independent writing.

All too often children are taught grammar, punctuation and vocabulary with exercises that aren't rooted within an authentic experience; and, as a result, although they may gain full marks in their exercise books, they often misapply or omit what has been learnt in their own free writing.

The *Top Class* series seeks to address this problem using a three staged approach, each Lesson Plan being structured so that learners are encouraged to investigate and explore the English language; initially with support and guidance from their teacher and fellow peers before being asked to apply what they have learnt as individuals.

Think about...
Before undertaking the Guided activity, learners are asked about what they already know about a particular piece of punctuation or grammatical form and where they might have seen it.

This links directly to the Guided text, again helping learners to view grammar, punctuation and vocabulary in context, housing it so that stronger links can be made with prior learning and personal experiences. This can then be used as a springboard to explore and develop this further in a familiar setting.

For example, when looking at our use of capital letters when writing a proper noun, learners may be asked about why people use an atlas or map before looking at a tourist map of London and considering why place names and famous tourist attractions start with a capital letter.

Guided
This is a shared activity that engages the whole class.

Set within a specific and relevant genre of Literacy, it embeds each particular piece of grammar, punctuation or vocabulary being taught in a focused and meaningful way. Moreover, it invites learners to use this information in order to answer a series of questions that are related to the text itself and then begins to move beyond it.

Each of the three questions asked have been carefully formatted so that valuable practice for the end of *Key Stage 2 English grammar, punctuation and spelling test* can be undertaken throughout each Year group. Marks are also available so that pupils gain practice at providing fuller explanations for those questions where two or three marks are being awarded. Answers are provided on the Lesson Plan.

Independent
This activity can be completed as an individual, with a partner or within a small group.

Each Independent activity within the book is also differentiated at an upper and lower level* and offers teachers a range of practical activities that support learners as they practice what they have learnt in the Guided section.

*Differentiated activities can be found on the CD Rom.

Homework

Included in this section is a homework activity that aims to encourage wider learning outside of the classroom to take place. There are two types of homework activities that are provided, each having been designed to help learners discover and engage with grammar, punctuation and vocabulary in the 'real' world:

A] Specific 'closed' questions may be asked in order that research skills, both modern and traditional, can be employed to find a particular answer.

For example: What is the capital city of Demark? Who was the first man to walk on the moon? When necessary, answers are provided on the Lesson Plan.

B] Wider 'open' tasks are given in order to afford learners the opportunity to explore the world around them and collect examples that are both pertinent and authentic.

For example, learners may be asked to find three examples where a shop's name uses an apostrophe in their local high street.

Extension

This final stage of the learning journey is an important one and underscores the importance of using a 'top-down' approach to the teaching and learning of grammar, punctuation and vocabulary.

Each Extension activity within the book is also differentiated at an upper and lower level.*

Its aim is to encourage children to apply what they have learnt in a meaningful and purposeful way in order to embed their learning.

For example, learners may be asked to write a shopping list when planning a party that will naturally include a colon or use strong adjectives to describe a certain event in a story.

More importantly, it is this *writing for purpose* (rather than to score arbitrary marks or achieve irrelevant ticks in an exercise book) that provides a meaningful opportunity for individuals to engage with the English language and create their own work that uses grammar, punctuation and vocabulary in a way that brings their work to life.

In this way, not only will each learner be encouraged to use particular forms of grammar, punctuation or vocabulary correctly but, essentially, they will gain a strong sense of themselves taking an active role as a writer. It gives them a valuable sense of what it is like to be an author, one who uses grammar not only to improve the quality of their work but also to express themselves as best they can using the written word.

The journey from simply understanding how the English language works to being able to apply that knowledge in order to become a capable and confident writer is a journey that will continue into adulthood and one that, in all truthfulness, never really ends.

However, by providing meaningful activities for both the classroom and beyond, the *Top Class* series can help each and every writer to freely use grammar, punctuation and vocabulary to great effect and support them as they endeavour to bring the written word to life in order to inform, influence and entertain their readers.

Differentiated activities can be found on the CD Rom.

Capital Letters

Think about...
What is an I.D. badge?
Why do people wear I.D. badges?
What information might you see on an I.D. badge?
What information would begin with a capital letter?
Why?

Guided

Imagine you are on the International Space Station.

Which astronaut would you like to talk to? Why? With a partner choose one to interview and write three questions you would like to ask them. What might their answer to each question be?

Once done, find another pair that want to interview the same astronaut and compare your questions. Then answer the questions on page 9.

Independent

Read the biography of the first man in space.

On your own, with a partner or in a small group; complete the task sheet provided to you by your teacher on page 10.

Once finished, cut off the homework task to take home with you for further practice.

Extension

Write a short fictional biography for the first person to walk on Mars. Complete the task sheet on page 11.

Once completed, design and make the I.D. badge they will need for their mission.

Answers

1 Youngest – Elizabeth Barnes
Oldest – Jasper Cohen

2 International Space Camp
Name: Louella **Tilly**
Date of Birth: 1st **November**, 1990
Place of Birth: Paris, **France**
Nationality: French
Name of Space Capsule: Raven 4

3 Peter – Name of a person
Germany – Name of a country
June – Name of a month

Homework

- Neil Armstrong, Ohio (USA)
- July 20th, 1969
- Edwin Eugene ("Buzz") Aldrin
- President Nixon

Remember...
We use **capital letters** for the names of people and places but also for days of the week and months of the year.

Capital Letters

International Space Camp

Name: Jasper Cohen
Date of Birth: 23rd April, 1968
Place of Birth: Texas, USA
Nationality: American
Name of Space Capsule: Griffin 6

International Space Camp

Name: Elizabeth Barnes
Date of Birth: 2nd February, 1985
Place of Birth: London, UK
Nationality: British
Name of Space Capsule: Pegasus 3

International Space Camp

Name: Dr X. Chang
Date of Birth: 12th August, 1977
Place of Birth: Beijing, China
Nationality: Chinese
Name of Space Capsule: Phoenix 2

Look at the I.D. badges and answer the questions below.

1 Who is the youngest and oldest astronaut?

Youngest:

Oldest:

2 marks

2 Correct this I.D. badge:

International Space Camp

Name: Louella tilly

Date of Birth: 1st november, 1990

Place of Birth: Paris, france

Nationality: French

Name of Space Capsule: Raven 4

International Space Camp

Name:

Date of Birth:

Place of Birth:

Nationality:

Name of Space Capsule:

3 marks

3 Why do these three words start with a capital letter?

Peter went to Germany for his holiday in June.

_____

_____

3 marks

TOP CLASS - Punctuation - Year 3

Capital Letters

Read this short biography about the first man in space. Use the information to fill in the I.D. badge below. Don't forget to use a capital letter when you need to.

Fact File:

Yuri Gagarin was born March 9th, 1934 in the village of Klushino, Russia. Later, the town next door (Gzhatsk) was renamed 'Gagarin' in his honour.

He was the third of four children and grew up to be a fighter pilot.

Yuri was one of twenty pilots chosen for Russia's space programme. He was so popular with his classmates that, when they were all asked to vote in secret for which one of them should become the first man in space, all but three chose him.

On April 12th, 1961 Yuri became the first human to go into space. His space capsule was called 'Vostok 1' and his flight lasted 108 minutes. He was now a true cosmonaut!*

When he returned to Earth, he used a parachute to land after ejecting from his space capsule. A local farmer and her daughter saw him dressed in his orange spacesuit and were so scared that it took him a few minutes to convince them he was Russian and to point him to the nearest telephone!

Yuri Gagarin became a national hero and statues were built across Russia to honour him. Sadly, he died in a plane crash on March 27th, 1968.

However, his bravery and name will live forever for being the first man ever to go into space.

*Cosmonaut is the Russian word for 'astronaut'.

ID Badge

Name: _____

Date of Birth: _____

Place of Birth: _____

Nationality: _____

Name of Space Capsule: _____

Homework

Find out about the first man to walk on the moon.
- What was his name? Where was he from?
- When did this event happen?
- Who was with him?
- Who did he telephone?

Capital Letters

You are the Captain of the first spaceship to travel to Mars! Write a short biography about one of the crew members travelling with you through space. What is their name? When and where were they born? What is the name of your spaceship?

Name: | **Date:**

Destination:

Crew Member:

Date of Birth:

Place of Birth:

Nationality:

Name of Spaceship:

Launch Date:

ID Badge

Name: _____

Date of Birth: _____

Place of Birth: _____

Nationality: _____

Name of Space Capsule: _____

Full Stops

Think about...
What is a telegram?
When were they used?
Why did they use short sentences?
What might you see on a telegram?

Guided

Imagine you are researching information about the Titanic.

You find some telegrams that were sent from and to the Titanic. Think about what is being said in each telegram and what it means. How are people feeling? Why are the sentences so short? Are there any words missing? Why?

Once done, answer the questions on page 13.

Independent

Read some telegrams sent by survivors of the Titanic disaster.

On your own, with a partner or in a small group; complete the task sheet provided to you by your teacher on page 14.

Once finished, cut off the homework task to take home with you for further practice.

Extension

Write a telegram to your family telling them you have been rescued from the Titanic. Complete the task sheet on page 15.

Once complete, look up some more interesting facts about the people who were travelling on the Titanic.

Answers

1
| One sentence = C |
| Two sentences = A,D |
| Three sentences = |
| Four sentences = B |

2 We are putting women and children in small boats.
(Allow for variations of this sentence)

3 Require immediate assistance. Come at once. We struck an iceberg. Sinking.

Homework

- Captain Edward John Smith
- The Carpathia
- Millvina Dean [9 weeks old]. She was also the last survivor of the disaster, passing away aged 97 in 2009.
- September 1st, 1985

Remember...
We use a **full stop** at the end of a sentence.

12   TOP CLASS - Punctuation - Year 3

Full Stops

On April 14th, 1912 at 11:40 pm, the Titanic struck an iceberg. Telegrams were sent to other ships to ask for help. 2 hours and 40 minutes later, she sank.

A
From: The Titanic
This is Titanic. Engine room flooded.

B
From: The Titanic
We are putting passengers off in small boats. Women and children in boats. Cannot last much longer. Losing power.

C
From: The Olympic
Am lighting up all boilers as fast as we can.

D
From: The Titanic
[Her final message]
Come quick. Engine room nearly full.

Look at the telegrams and answer the questions below.

1 Fill in the table below.

One sentence	Two sentences	Three sentences	Four sentences

3 marks

2 Look at telegram B. Write a single sentence to replace the first two sentences.

_____
_____
_____

2 marks

3 Put full stops in the telegram below.

[Sent: April 15th, 12:17 am]
Require immediate assistance Come at once We struck an iceberg Sinking

4 marks

TOP CLASS - Punctuation - Year 3

Full Stops

Read about how one family from Guernsey waited to see if their loved one had survived the sinking of the Titanic. Put a full stop in this recount when you need to. There are eight missing.

A Recount :

Gerald Duquemin takes up the story:

"I was only ten years old at the time the Titanic went down but I can remember very well what results the sinking brought home. We heard about it on the 15th or 16th of April but there was no news of my brother. I remember my mother was so shocked and worried we had to have the doctor (he used to come on horseback) and he confined my mother to bed. We all waited for news. Mother said she had a feeling Joseph was all right but as time went by, we began to fear the worst

Then on April 20th (my mother's birthday) Mr Veal of the Post Office arrived in father's building yard Mr Veal came himself with the telegram He wouldn't send one of the boys I remember my father coming towards the house with the telegram in his hands They were shaking so much he couldn't read the words He called to my sister to read them out There were only five words: Joseph Duquemin reported safe, Ismay"

Homework

Find out about the Titanic.
- Who was the Captain of the Titanic?
- Which ship rescued the Titanic survivors?
- Who was the youngest survivor?
- When was the wreck discovered?

Full Stops

You are a survivor of the Titanic. Write a telegram to your family and tell them you are safe. What will you say? Will you ask them to bring anything for you? How many words will you use? Why?
How might your family reply?

Name: **Date:**

A

B

Question Marks

Think about...
Why might detectives ask questions?
What questions might they ask when investigating a robbery?
Is there ever a time when we might ask a question and don't need an answer?

Guided

Imagine you are an actor learning your lines for a play.

What do you expect your script to look like? How can you tell that this is a script and not a story book? Discuss and share your ideas with a partner and practice this scene together.

Once done, perform your scene for another pair and watch their performance too. How do they compare? Then answer the questions on page 17.

Independent

You are the writer of this play and are writing a new scene.

On your own, with a partner or in a small group; complete the task sheet provided to you by your teacher on page 18.

Once finished, cut off the homework task to take home with you for further practice.

Extension

Write a new scene for this play. Complete the task on page 19.

Once completed, find a partner and act your new scene out!

Answers

1 1 2 3 4 [5]

2 "At what time was the necklace last seen**?**" Inspector Doyle asks. Nobody answers.

3 **Who** saw the necklace last night?
How much is the necklace worth?
When did the necklace go missing?
Where (allow for personal response)

Homework

- No specific answers are required for this task, though teachers should check that the questions provided for this scene by the learner make sense and the use of their question mark is applied correctly.

Remember...
We use a **question mark** at the end of a question to show that a question has been asked, whether we want the question answered or not.

16   TOP CLASS - Punctuation - Year 3

Question Marks

Act I, Scene III

Setting: *The library at Mulberry Hall. The sun hangs low in the sky and everywhere is hushed. The oak door creaks slowly open.*

PC Haines: [Scratching his head] How do you think he got in? All the doors and windows are locked and the fireplace is still warm!

Inspector Doyle: He? What makes you think the thief is a he? Diamonds are a girl's best friend after all you know.

[The clock strikes seven]

Inspector Doyle: We're missing something Haines. How is it possible for a room to be locked from the inside yet nobody be in it when the door is later unlocked from the outside? And, more importantly, why would somebody steal a necklace so famous that they would never be able to wear it?

Look at the play script and answer the questions below.

1 How many questions are asked in this scene?

1   2   3   4   5

1 mark

2 Tick one box to show where the missing question mark should go.

"At what time was the necklace last seen" Inspector Doyle asks. Nobody answers.

1 mark

3 Draw a line to complete each of the following questions.
Write your own question for the one that has no answer.

Who   is the necklace worth?

How much   did the necklace go missing?

When   saw the necklace last night?

Where   _____

4 marks

TOP CLASS - Punctuation - Year 3

Question Marks

You are writing the scene where Inspector Doyle asks Lady Mulberry about the disappearance of her necklace. Look at how she answers and think of a good question for the Inspector to ask. Don't forget to use a question mark after each question you ask.

Act II, Scene V

Setting:	*The Study. The wind is blowing the curtains. Lady Mulberry walks over and closes the window.*
Inspector Doyle:	_____
Lady Mulberry:	No, I'm fine. I'd rather stand. I didn't sleep well last night so if I sit down I'll probably fall asleep.
Inspector Doyle:	_____
Lady Mulberry:	In bed of course. Apart from when I went to the kitchen.
Inspector Doyle:	_____
Lady Mulberry:	I needed to get a glass of cold water. I had a headache and wanted to take some tablets.
Inspector Doyle:	_____
Lady Mulberry:	It was 4am. I know because I heard the grandfather clock chime as I was running the tap.
Inspector Doyle:	_____
Lady Mulberry:	Nobody Inspector. I was quite alone.
Inspector Doyle:	_____
Lady Mulberry:	Yes of course I did. I put the necklace in the safe myself. And before you ask...no, I was quite alone when I did that too!

Homework

Write the next scene for this play, when Inspector Doyle is questioning the butler about the stolen necklace. What questions do you think he would ask the butler? How might the butler answer?

Question Marks

You are writing one of the last scenes of the play. It is where Inspector Doyle is questioning Lord Mulberry about the stolen necklace. Where in Mulberry Hall will you set this scene? What questions will you get the Inspector to ask? How will Lord Mulberry reply? Will you add stage directions to this scene? If so, what will they be?

Name: **Date:**

Act X, Scene VIII

Setting:

Inspector Doyle:

Lord Mulberry:

Inspector Doyle:

Lord Mulberry:

Inspector Doyle:

Lord Mulberry:

Inspector Doyle:

Lord Mulberry:

Inspector Doyle:

Lord Mulberry:

TOP CLASS - Punctuation - Year 3

Exclamation Marks

Think about...
Look at this sentence: It was amazing.
How might you read this out loud?
Now look at this sentence: It was amazing!
How has this sentence changed? Which is stronger?
How might this affect your reading? Why?

Guided

You are reading a book entitled 'Our Solar System' for a school project.

Do you think this book will be factual or fictional? Why? What types of words and numbers might it contain? What information would you expect to find in such a book? Do you know any interesting facts about our solar system?

Once done, share them with your classmates. Then answer the questions on page 21.

Independent

Use your research skills to find out some amazing facts about another planet in our solar system.

On your own, with a partner or in a small group; complete the task sheet provided to you by your teacher on page 22.

Once finished, cut off the homework task to take home with you for further practice.

Extension

Write a postcard telling friends about your holiday on an amazing planet...Earth! Complete the task sheet on page 23.

Once completed, make a Top Ten list of the most interesting facts about our planet you can find!

Answers

1 Wow!

2 The sun is huge! The writer is astonished by how many Earths will fit into the sun and its colossal size. The word 'huge' is made stronger by using an exclamation mark.

3 Stop!   Fantastic!

Homework

- Our solar system has only 8 planets. In 2006, scientists declared Pluto too small to be classed as a true planet.

- Jupiter: its radius is 69, 911km compared with Earth's 6, 371km.

- Mercury: It is just short of 58 million km from the sun compared with Earth's average distance being 93 million km.

- Mars: also known as the Red Planet because of its red, blood coloured soil.

Remember...
We use an **exclamation mark** to show an intense sense of emotion; especially when following a command. When used at the end of a sentence, it can imply that what is written is of incredible interest or astonishment to the writer and, possibly, the reader too.

Exclamation Marks

The Sun
- Our sun is huge! Almost 1,000,000 Earths would fit inside it.
- Light from the sun takes 8 minutes and 20 seconds to reach us.

The Moon
- The moon is moving away from us at approximately 3.8 cm per year!
- Because the moon has no atmosphere, there is no sound and the sky is always black.

The Earth
- Wow! From a distance, Earth would be the brightest planet in our solar system due to the sun's rays reflecting off its watery surface.

- Earth's name, unlike the other planets that are named after Roman gods and goddesses, comes from the Anglo-Saxon word '*erda*' meaning *ground* or *soil*, despite 71% of it being covered in water.

Look at this book about space and answer the questions below.

1 Which word uses an exclamation mark to show the writer thinks this fact about Earth is amazing?

1 mark

2 Which of the two sun facts does the writer think is the most interesting? Why?

_____

_____

2 marks

3 Which two words are most likely to be followed by an exclamation mark?

Stop   Who   Perhaps   When   Fantastic   However

2 marks

TOP CLASS - Punctuation - Year 3

Exclamation Marks

Use your research skills to find some fascinating facts about a planet in our solar system. Put each of your facts into a separate box below. Don't forget to use an exclamation mark to show the reader you think your fact is truly amazing!

Planet:

Homework
Use your research skills to find the following:
- How many planets are there in our solar system?
- Which is the biggest planet?
- Which is the closest planet to the sun?
- Which planet is named after the Roman god of war?

Exclamation Marks

You are an alien visiting Earth for a holiday! Write a postcard about this wonderful destination. What is interesting about this strange new world? What do you find amazing about this planet? Why might your alien friends want to visit too?

Name: **Date:**

Commas (within lists)

Think about...
What do you think a list poem is?
What sorts of things do you think you would find in a list poem? Why? Do you think you would see any commas in a list poem? Why?
Why do people use commas when writing a list?

Guided

Imagine you are on a hill watching the clouds pass by on a summer's day.

What might the clouds look like? Draw three things your mind's eye might see in the clouds above.

Once done, choose your favourite one to show the class and explain why it is your favourite. Then answer the questions on page 25.

Independent

You want to use your imagination to write a list poem.

On your own, with a partner or in a small group; complete the task sheet provided to you by your teacher on page 26.

Once finished, cut off the homework task to take home with you for further practice.

Extension

Write the first draft of your list poem. Complete the task on page 27.

Once completed, publish your list poem on a computer!

Answers

1. 8 [A dragon, a ghost, a monster's claw, a pirate, a spaceship, a dinosaur's roar, an angel and a rabbit]

2. An angle, a dinosaur's roar, a dragon, a ghost, a monster's claw, a pirate, a rabbit and a spaceship

3. b) A kitten, a snowman and a bowl of ice cream.

Homework

- No specific answers are required for this task, though teachers should check that the lists provided by each learner have included the necessary commas and use of 'and'.

Remember...
We use a **comma** when we are writing a list to show a break between each different item in that list. However, the last two items in the list use 'and' between them instead of a comma.

Commas (within lists)

CLOUD SCAPES

As I lay on a sea of green, clouds drifted lazily by,

And with my mind's eye,

I painted pictures in the heavens above:

A dragon, a ghost and a monster's claw,

A pirate, a spaceship and a dinosaur's ROAR!

An angel, a rabbit and then came the sun,

One moment they lived and the next they were gone.

Read the list poem and answer the questions below.

1 How many pictures does the poet paint with his mind's eye?

| 1 | 2 | 3 | 4 | 5 | 6 | 7 | 8 | 9 | 10 |

1 mark

2 Write down the list in alphabetical order.

_____

_____

_____

3 marks

3 Which list is punctuated correctly?

a) **A kitten, a snowman, a bowl of ice cream.**

b) **A kitten, a snowman and a bowl of ice cream.**

1 mark

TOP CLASS - Punctuation - Year 3

Commas (within lists)

You decide to write a list poem called 'The Song of the Shadows'. Make a list of ideas for your first draft. Don't forget to use a comma between each shadow you see and remember to use 'and' between the last two.

THE SONG OF THE SHADOWS

As I lay in my bed, the darkness crept in,
And the song of the shadows did gently begin.

On top of the bookshelf: _____

Behind the toy box: _____

In the corner by the window: _____

Beneath the bed: _____

Homework

Write a list under the following subjects:
- Three flavours of ice cream you would like to eat
- Four creatures you might spot in a garden pond
- Five planets you can find in outer space
- Six countries you would like to visit in Europe

Commas (within lists)

Now that you have collected some ideas for your list poem, begin to put them together to write your first draft. What mysterious things lurk in the darkness around you? What shapes do you see in the shadows beyond?

Name: **Date:**

THE SONG OF THE SHADOWS

As I lay in my bed, the darkness crept in,
And the song of the shadows did gently begin.

TOP CLASS - Punctuation - Year 3

Commas (within clauses)

Think about...
Look at this sentence: Brad put down his pencil glad that the test was over. Where should the comma go? Why? Colour the two parts: What Brad does (blue). How Brad feels (red). Write the sentence so that the two clauses switch around.

Guided

You are reading the diary of a Victorian vampire hunter.

What things might they have with them for protection? What nocturnal animal might you see that is associated with this monster? Draw your answers.

Once done, share your ideas with your teacher. Then answer the questions on page 29.

Independent

You are asked to help a friend do their homework.

On your own, with a partner or in a small group; complete the task sheet provided to you by your teacher on page 30.

Once finished, cut off the homework task to take home with you for further practice.

Extension

Write a ghost story to tell around a campfire to scare your friends. Complete the task on page 31.

Once completed, submit it into a class competition and vote for your favourite.

Answers

1 April 5th, 2004

2 a) 100,000
b) 8,000,000
c) 31,536,000

3 I. I clasped my hands together, whispering one final prayer before the battle began.
II. Whispering one final prayer before the battle began, I clasped my hands together.

Homework

- No specific answers are required for this task, though teachers should check that the sentences provided for this task make sense and the use of the comma is applied correctly.

Remember...
We use a **comma** to break a long sentence into two parts to make it easier to read. We also use a comma in this way to break up long numbers and when writing long dates.

Commas (within clauses)

> May 15th, 1895 and I (Lucy Barker, a humble parlour maid) lay in my bed wide awake. I knew the vampire was coming. I had seen the bat flying by my window the night before. But I was not scared. I had garlic in my pockets and a crucifix around my neck. Beneath my pillow I'd hidden a small wooden stake. Tonight I would end this nightmare...for good! I gazed at the 1,000,000 stars that lit up the night sky. Suddenly, there came a tapping on the window and I knew it was time. I clasped my hands together whispering one final prayer before the battle began.

Look at this diary extract and answer the questions below.

1 Circle the date that is written correctly.

June 12th 1923   April 5th, 2004   March, 19th 1986   August, 2nd, 2009

1 mark

2 Put the commas in the following numbers:

a) **Unless they are bald, people have around 100000 hairs growing on their head!**

b) **There are around 8000000 words in the English language and growing!**

c) **There are 31536000 seconds in a year!**

3 marks

3 The final sentence is missing a comma. Where should it go?
Rewrite this sentence by switching the order of the two clauses?

I. _____

II. _____

2 marks

Commas (within clauses)

You want to help your friend Samir do his homework. Look at each sentence and colour the two parts different colours. Don't forget to add a comma to show where the two clauses meet.

Colour 1: ☐ *What do they do?*   **Colour 2:** ☐ *How do they feel?*

1. Alice began to cry sad that she wouldn't see her dad again for another year.

2. Billy laughed out loud happy that Sally Grimshaw had finally come 2nd in a Spelling Test.

3. The cow lay down knowing that it was soon about to rain.

4. Gary put on his safety helmet and boots nervous about the mountain climb ahead.

5. Lucy threw away her umbrella angry that she was about to get soaked.

6. Anthony held his breath scared that the monster would hear him breathing.

Rewrite these sentences so that the two clauses swap order.

--➤

Homework

Find out about your favourite monster.
- What book are they found in? Who wrote it? When?
- Do they appear in any famous films?
- What does this monster look like? How do they act?
- Where do they live? How are they killed?

Commas (within clauses)

You are a monster hunter! Create a Wanted poster. Who do you want to catch? Why do you want to catch them? Will there be a reward? Where was it last seen? What was it doing? What does it look like? Do you need to warn the reader of anything?

Name: **Date:**

Wanted Dead or Alive!

Inverted Commas

Think about...
Look at this sentence:
'What was that?' said Paul.
Who is speaking here? What does he say?
How do we show this using inverted commas?
What is another term we use for inverted commas?

Guided

Imagine you are reading a story to your younger brother or sister.

How might you use your voice to show how different characters speak? What voice would you use for the following: an old man, an angry giant, a tiny mouse, a witch, a lion? Why?

Once done, share your ideas with another group and act out the voice you have chosen for each character. What might each character say?

Then answer the questions on page 33.

Independent

You are looking at various characters from different children's books.

On your own, with a partner or in a small group; complete the task sheet provided to you by your teacher on page 34.

Once finished, cut off the homework task to take home with you for further practice.

Extension

Rewrite a well known fable. Retell Aesop's story of the mouse and the lion. Complete the task sheet on page 35.

Once completed, why not read your fable to someone in Year 2!

Answers

1 Blue
Red
Blue
Red
Yellow

2 Jane

3 "Some dogs," said the owner of the pet shop, "are used to help people".

Homework

- No specific answers are required for this task, though teachers should check that the conversation provided by each learner has included the necessary speech marks.

Remember...
We use **inverted commas** (or **speech marks**) to show which words are being spoken.

Inverted Commas

She huffed.

"Are you sure you know where you buried it? We've been digging for nearly an hour and found nothing but a half eaten shoe and a piece of china."

"Look! It's definitely close by. I remember sheltering under that willow tree when it began raining and watched as an empty hole became a muddy puddle."

"And you're certain it was *that* willow tree and not another?" she asked, not expecting a sensible answer.

"Yes! 100%! I remember that branch. You know; the one that was hit by lightning last September."

Just then the back door opened and Jane stood there with two leads and a tennis ball in her hand.

"Come on you two, time for walkies."

Their buried treasure would have to wait.

Read this extract from a children's story and answer the questions below.

1 Colour the speech for each of the three characters:

Blue = Character 1   **Red = Character 2**   **Yellow = Jane**

3 marks

2 Which character speaks last?

1 mark

3 Insert the missing inverted commas in the sentence below.

Some dogs, said the owner of the pet shop, are used to help people.

2 marks

TOP CLASS - Punctuation - Year 3

Inverted Commas

You are planning to write a story for younger children. What might each of these characters say in your story? How would they say it? Write their words in the speech bubble. Don't forget to add speech marks when you write their words on the line below.

What did they say?

_____ cackled the witch

_____ bellowed the giant

_____ squeaked the mouse

_____ whispered the ghost

_____ moaned the king

_____ roared the lion

_____ yelled the teacher

_____ screamed mum

Homework

Read Aesop's fable *The Lion and the Mouse*.
Draw a picture of the lion and the mouse.
What do they say to each other when they meet?
How do they say it?
Write out their conversation.

Inverted Commas

Retell the Aesop fable of *The Lion and the Mouse* for young children. How do the two animals meet? How does the mouse help the lion? How does the lion help the mouse? Why do they become friends? What is the moral of this tale?

Name: **Date:**

Once upon a time...

Moral

Apostrophes (for omission)

Think about...
How might you write to a friend?
Would you use formal or informal words?
Why? Which is more informal:
I am or I'm? Can you give some more examples?
How is the apostrophe used to make this informal?

Guided

Imagine you have received an email from a friend.

With a partner, make a list of things you might expect to see in your email. How might the email start? How might it end? What might the email be about? Will it be long or short? What type of language will be used? What else might you see?

Once done, share your ideas with your classmates.
Then answer the questions on page 37.

Independent

You want to write an email to Laura.

On your own, with a partner or in a small group; complete the task sheet provided to you by your teacher on page 38.

Once finished, cut off the homework task to take home with you for further practice.

Extension

Write an email to a friend inviting them to go to the cinema. Complete the task on page 39.

Once complete, send your email to a classmate and wait for their response!

Answers

1 Informal

2 The following answer must have been considered to award a mark:
- It uses lots of informal words that are joined together with an apostrophe (contractions).
- Either one of the following:
It begins with 'Hi'
It uses the name Steph

3

I am / I'm	it is / it's
will not / won't *	can not / can't
I will / I'll	he is / he's

Irregular

Homework

- No specific answers are required for this task, though teachers should check the examples collected by each learner. Particular attention may be required here in order that learners do not provide examples that show the use of an apostrophe indicating possession.

Remember...
We use an **apostrophe** to join two words together.
This is informal so we often use this when writing to family or friends.

Apostrophes (for omission)

Inbox (37)
Drafts
Sent
Spam (12)
Trash

To: steph@talktalk.net
CC:
Subject: **Football on Saturday**

Hi Steph,
I'm really looking forward to playing football on Saturday. It's supposed to be beautiful all weekend so we won't get muddy like last time! I can't find my boots though so I'll have to borrow some from Jack. He's not going to be happy, LOL.
See you soon,
Laura

Look at this email and answer the questions below.

1 Is this email formal or informal?

☐ Formal   ☐ Informal

1 mark

2 Give two reasons why you think this.

I. _____

II. _____

2 marks

3 There are six words here that use an apostrophe to join two words together. List them.

Put a star ★ next to the odd one out.

Formal	Informal

3 marks

TOP CLASS - Punctuation - Year 3

Apostrophes (for omission)

You read the first draft of your email to Laura and realise it is too formal. Write a second draft underneath. Don't forget to use an apostrophe to contract two words together when necessary.

Inbox (1)
Drafts
Sent
Spam
Trash

To: laura@talktalk.net
CC:
Subject: **RE: Football on Saturday**

Hi Laura,
I am really sorry but I can not play football on Saturday. It is my brother's birthday and we are going out for the day to the zoo. He is really excited! I will call you on Sunday. Do you want to go to the cinema? I have won two tickets to watch Spiderman so it will not cost you anything (apart from a hot dog and some popcorn for me – LOL). My mum says she will pick us up after so you do not need to worry about getting home.
Speak soon,
Steph

Homework

Go on an apostrophe hunt!
Find ten examples of when two words have been joined together using an apostrophe.
Make a list of where you found each example and think about how you would write it formally as two words.

Apostrophes (for omission)

Write an email to a friend inviting them to go to the cinema with you. What film do you want to see? What time does it start? Where do you want to meet? When? Do they need to bring anything? How will you get home?

Name:	Date:

Use the checklist below to help you write your email on the computer.

My Email to a friend – A Checklist:

☐ I start my email with 'Hi'.

☐ I use my friend's first name only (or their nick name).

☐ I put a comma after their name.

☐ I tell my friend why I am writing my email.

☐ I give my friend details about meeting up. This includes:

  ☐ What film we will be watching.

  ☐ The time the film starts.

  ☐ Where and when we will meet.

  ☐ If they should bring anything (food, drink or 3D glasses).

  ☐ How we will get home.

☐ I end my email with an informal phrase.

☐ ☐ I sign off with my first name and use an emoticon.

TOP CLASS - Punctuation - Year 3

Apostrophes (for possession)

Think about...
When you go shopping, what kind of shops might you visit? What would you buy from them? For who? Who might own these shops? How would the shop's sign indicate this? How would an apostrophe be used to show this?

Guided

Imagine you are walking down your local High Street.

Choose a shop you would like to visit. Think about the name of the person who owns the shop. Draw a sign for the shop and include their name.

Once done, share your sign with your classmates. Together, create your own local High Street full of different shops. Then answer the questions on page 41.

Independent

You are asked to tidy your bedroom.

On your own, with a partner or in a small group; complete the task sheet provided to you by your teacher on page 42.

Once finished, cut off the homework task to take home with you for further practice.

Extension

Write a story about the day you moved house. Complete the task on page 43.

Once done, publish your story on the computer!

Answers

1 A wedding cake: Brenda's Bakery
A wedding ring: Jess' Jewellery
A wedding bouquet: Florence's Florist

2 Sally's Sweet Shop
Chris' Clothes Shop

3 B] Lizzy's Café

Homework

- No specific answers are required for this task, though teachers should check the examples provided by each learner.

Remember...
We add an **apostrophe** ('s) to show possession.
If a person's name already ends with an 's' then we don't need to add the s and can just use an apostrophe on its own.

Apostrophes (for possession)

Billy's Birds *Your feathered friends at cheap, cheap prices!*	*Brenda's Bakery* Buns and bread, bakes and cakes for all occasions
Chloe's Charity Shop Small change can make a big difference!	Gary's Grocery Your five a day, the fruit and veg way.
Florence's Florist *Whatever you say, say it with flowers.*	Elsa's Electricals FOR ALL YOUR WHITE GOODS AND MORE
Colin's Comedy Club (capes not included)	Jess' Jewellery Because 'I love you' sounds better with a diamond.

Look at the shop signs and answer the questions below.

1 Whose shop would you visit to buy the following items?

A wedding cake: _____

A wedding ring: _____

A wedding bouquet: _____

3 marks

2 Put an apostrophe in each shop sign.

Sallys Sweet Shop	Chris Clothes Shop

2 marks

3 Which sign is written correctly?

A. Lizzys Café	B. Lizzy's Café	C. Lizzys' Café

1 mark

TOP CLASS - Punctuation - Year 3

Apostrophes (for possession)

You are asked to tidy your bedroom and put your toys away. However, not all the toys you find belong to you. Whose toys do you find? Where do you find them? Use an apostrophe to show who owns which toy. Make a list of whose toy you found and where you found it.

Where did you find it?

1. Peter's teddy bear was next to the wardrobe.
2.
3.
4.
5.
6.
7.
8.

under the bed   beneath the window
                 beside the door
next to the wardrobe ✓

cricket bat
                                   football
    teddy bear ✓

         Imran   Jasmin
doll   Chris   Tess   toy
         Peter ✓ Fiona   rocket
         Abdul   Lilly

yo-yo   skate board
      tennis racket

on the rug
            inside the drawers
in front of the TV   behind the curtains

Homework

You want to buy a present for each member of your family. Draw the present you would like to buy and label it, showing who it belongs to. Think about which shop you would buy each present from and design a sign for each one.

42   TOP CLASS - Punctuation - Year 3

Apostrophes (for possession)

Write a story about the day you moved house. What things needed to be moved? Who did they belong to? What happened to them? Was anything lost? Was anything broken? Was anything found?

Name: **Date:**

My Moving Day

Empty boxes lined up in front of us like cardboard monsters waiting to be fed, their mouths opened wide ready to gobble up anything we placed inside their toothless mouths. The removal van was on its way and we still hadn't finished packing!

Brackets

Think about...
Look at this sentence: Jack was an old man.
What might a writer want to tell us about Jack?
Where might they put this extra information?
Now look at this: Jack (74) was an old man.
Why do you think this writer uses brackets here?

Guided

Imagine you have visited Jack in the old people's home.

Who might the character of Jack be? Why do you think this? Be a Reading Detective and highlight any clues that might suggest who Jack really is.

Once done, share your ideas with your classmates. Then answer the questions on page 45.

Independent

Think about different characters you might find in fairy tales.

On your own, with a partner or in a small group; complete the task sheet provided to you by your teacher on page 46.

Once finished, cut off the homework task to take home with you for further practice.

Extension

Write a diary extract about when you met the gingerbread man. Complete the task on page 47.

Once completed, design your own gingerbread man and look for a recipe to make him!

Answers

1 Brown = (who had always loved playing in the garden as a little boy)
Green = (thinking of times long, long ago and far, far away)
Yellow = (much like the daffodils)

2 (who had always loved playing in the garden as a little boy)

3 Jack (who was 74 years old) was still as strong as an ox.

Homework

- No specific answers are required for this task, though teachers should check that the sentencess provided by each learner have included the necessary brackets.

Remember...
Writers use **brackets** when they want to give the reader extra information in a sentence but also want to keep it separate. If the information inside the bracket was removed, the sentence would still make sense.

Brackets

Old Jack

Jack (who had always loved playing in the garden as a little boy) was now old; old but not frail. He loved sitting in the garden of the old people's home, listening to the birds sing and watching the butterflies flutter by. The tulips, the bluebells and the daffodils all waved in the gentle breeze and a golden happiness (much like the daffodils) stirred deep within his heart.

A grumble of thunder could be heard in the distance and Jack (thinking of times long, long ago and far, far away) began to smile. He looked down at the seed packet labelled 'Runner Beans' he now held in his hands. 'Ah,' he chuckled, 'those were the days' and he began to tuck into his egg sandwich.

Look at this character study and answer the questions below.

1 Colour the three brackets in the text above as follows:

Brown	Tells us about Jack's childhood.
Green	Tells us about what Jack is thinking.
Yellow	Likens his happy heart to a flower.

3 marks

2 Which of these brackets is written in the past tense?

_____

_____

1 mark

3 Put brackets in this sentence.

Jack who was 74 years old was still as strong as an ox.

1 mark

Brackets

This is no ordinary old people's home. Soon you discover that many of the people who live here are from fairy tales. Look at the sentences below and add extra information about each character you meet. Don't forget to put this information inside brackets.

Who is it?		
Lucy put on her wolf skin coat and walked out the door.		(or 'Little Red' as she was better known)
She had always disliked apples so she chose the cheese and biscuits instead.		(especially the red ones)
Washing, drying and combing her hair took an age.		(which she always tied up in a plait)
The wicked witch sat by the fire.		(who, after all this time, still only wore black)
Size 22 boots were hard to find.		(the type that were sturdy enough for climbing down beanstalks)

Homework

Draw the big bad wolf and write three things about him. Place a piece of extra information (in brackets) about him in each of your sentences to make each one more interesting.

Brackets

You meet the gingerbread man as you are walking by the river. Write in your diary about what happened when you met him. What did he look like? How did he speak? What did he do? Did you see anyone nearby? Who where they? What happened next?

Name: **Date:**

My Diary

Yesterday I met a funny little man made out of gingerbread.

Ellipses

Think about...
How do fairy tales usually end?
How do soap operas usually end?
How are the two endings different?
Which would most likely end with 3 dots? Why?
What do we call these dots?

Guided

Imagine you are on holiday reading a book while you relax on the beach.

The chapter you are reading ends with a cliff hanger. What do you think this phrase means? Where do you think this phrase comes from? Why do you think writers use them? With a partner, jot down your ideas on some paper.

Once done, share your ideas with your teacher. Then answer the questions on page 49.

> The phrase 'cliff hanger' comes from the weekly adventure silent films of the early 1900s, where an episode would end with a main character being in immanent danger to ensure cinema goers would come back the following week to see how they escaped from their peril.

Independent

You are a writer who wants to end a chapter of your story with a cliff hanger.

On your own, with a partner or in a small group; complete the task sheet provided to you by your teacher on page 50.

Once finished, cut off the homework task to take home with you for further practice.

Extension

Write a cliff hanger ending and complete the task on page 51.

Once completed, practise reading your cliff hanger out loud to a friend!

Answers

1 At the end of a chapter

2 1 2 [3] 4 5

3 a] The writer has finished the chapter.
   d] The writer wants the reader to read the next chapter to find out what happens next.

Homework

- No specific answers are required for this task, though teachers should check that learners have correctly understood what a cliff hanger is and why soap operas use them to good effect.

Remember...
We use **ellipses** (...) when we want to show that a word or phrase is missing at the end of a story to create a cliff hanger. It makes the reader ask 'What will happen next?'

Ellipses

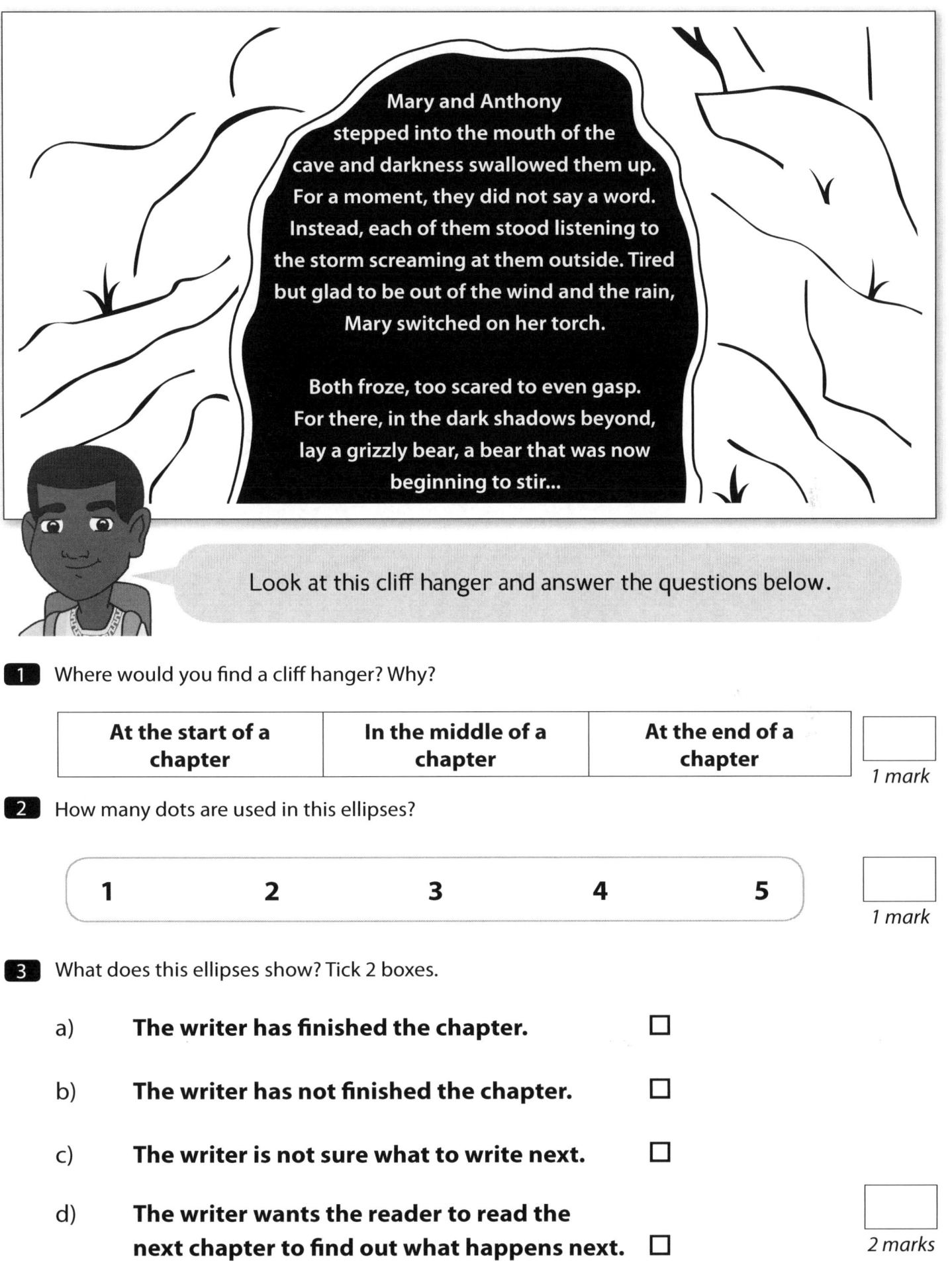

> Mary and Anthony stepped into the mouth of the cave and darkness swallowed them up. For a moment, they did not say a word. Instead, each of them stood listening to the storm screaming at them outside. Tired but glad to be out of the wind and the rain, Mary switched on her torch.
>
> Both froze, too scared to even gasp. For there, in the dark shadows beyond, lay a grizzly bear, a bear that was now beginning to stir...

Look at this cliff hanger and answer the questions below.

1 Where would you find a cliff hanger? Why?

At the start of a chapter	In the middle of a chapter	At the end of a chapter

1 mark

2 How many dots are used in this ellipses?

1	2	3	4	5

1 mark

3 What does this ellipses show? Tick 2 boxes.

a) **The writer has finished the chapter.** ☐

b) **The writer has not finished the chapter.** ☐

c) **The writer is not sure what to write next.** ☐

d) **The writer wants the reader to read the next chapter to find out what happens next.** ☐

2 marks

TOP CLASS - Punctuation - Year 3

Ellipses

You are writing an adventure story called 'Quest for the Golden Tiger'. You want to end Chapter Six with a cliff hanger. Here are some of your ideas. Choose your favourite one and make it into a cliff hanger using ellipses.

Quest for the Golden Tiger

A There, on top of a heap of seaweed, sat an old wooden box, beside it a large iron key. 'That's way too easy,' whispered Anthony. 'Do you think it's a trap?'

B A rusty sign hung on the wall, a skull and crossbones declaring 'DANGER! NO ENTRY!' Was this sign real or had it been put there by somebody trying to stop them finding out the truth? Both looked at each other, took a deep breath and walked deeper into the cave.

C A skeleton hung from the ceiling, a warning of what would befall anyone who dared look to for Blackbeard's treasure. Suddenly, footsteps echoed in the distance. Jumping behind a rock, Mary plunged her and Anthony back into darkness.

☙ Chapter Six ❧

_____
_____
_____
_____
_____
_____

Homework

Watch an episode of a soap opera of your choice. Think about how it ends. Write down three questions the viewer is left asking that will encourage them to watch the next episode.

Ellipses

Write a cliff hanger for Hansel and Gretel, when they discover that the old woman in the gingerbread house is in fact a witch.
How will you end this part of your story? Why?
What will it make your readers want to do next?

Name: **Date:**

❧ Chapter Four ❦

Colons

Think about...
Why do people write shopping lists?
Where do they often write them? How are they written? Where would they most likely read them? What might you do with this list when you got home? Why?

Guided

Imagine you are planning a birthday party for a friend.

What things might you want to buy for the party? With a partner, make a list of things you think you will need. Give your list sub-headings such as Food & Drink, Decorations, Party Games etc to help you.

Once done, find another pair who are planning the party and compare your lists. Then answer the questions on page 53.

Independent

Think about the games you are going to play at Ben's party.

On your own, with a partner or in a small group; complete the task sheet provided to you by your teacher on page 54.

Once finished, cut off the homework task to take home with you for further practice.

Extension

Plan a Sports Day for your school to help raise money for a local charity. Complete the task sheet on page 55.

Once completed, create a poster to advertise your special day!

Answers

1 1 2 [3] 4 5

2 Things to do

3 People to invite: Peter, Sarah, James, Charlie, Elijah, Narinda and Jess.
We put the colon here to show that we are going to write a list.

Homework

- No specific answers are required for this task, though teachers should check that the lists provided by each learner have included the necessary colons.

Remember...
We use a **colon** to show that we are going to write a list.

Colons

Things to do
Buy Ben's present
Write out his card
Put up decorations
Phone Claire for CD player
Clean BBQ
Games to play:
Musical chairs
Pass the parcel
Bob for apples
Pin the tail on the donkey

Things to buy:
A birthday cake
8 candles
16 muffins
12 beef burgers
4 vegetarian burgers
2 packets of frozen chips
3 large onions
Cheese slices
Bottle of ketchup
1/2 dozen tomatoes
2 lettuces
2 bags of apples (1 red, 1 green)

Look at the shopping list and answer the questions below.

1 How many lists have been written?

| 1 | 2 | 3 | 4 | 5 |

1 mark

2 Which sub-heading is missing a colon?

_____

1 mark

3 Put a colon in this sentence. Why have you put it here?

People to invite Peter, Sarah, James, Charlie, Elijah, Narinda and Jess.

_____
_____
_____

2 marks

TOP CLASS - Punctuation - Year 3

Colons

You are planning to play some games at Ben's birthday party. What equipment will you need for each one? Make a list for each of the games below. Don't forget to use a colon before you start each list.

Musical Chairs

_____
_____
_____
_____

Bob for Apples

_____
_____
_____
_____

_____
_____
_____
_____
_____

Pin the Tail on the Donkey

_____
_____
_____
_____

Pass the Parcel

_____
_____
_____
_____

Homework

You want to bake Ben's birthday cake for the party. Write a shopping list of ingredients you will need to buy and equipment you will need to use. Go to a supermarket and price up your ingredients. What is your total cost? Would it be cheaper to buy a birthday cake instead?

Colons

You are planning a Sports Day at your school to raise money for a local charity that helps disabled children play sport. Write a list of things you need to do, equipment (and refreshments) you will need to collect, people you would like to invite and activities you want to play.

Name: **Date:**

Our School's Sports Day

A

B

C

D

Semi-colons

Think about...
Put the following marks in order of pause length (. , ;) Which mark goes in the middle? Why? Where does it go in this sentence:
The rabbit was very ill the vet was called immediately.
Why do you think it goes here?

Guided

Imagine it is the first day of term after the summer holidays....and you're late!

Explain to your teacher why you are late. Did aliens attack you on the way to school? Did you rescue a dog from a burning building? Did you fall down a grid into an alternate universe?

Once you have your excuse, tell your teacher and answer the questions on page 57.

Independent

Your teacher has asked you to complete an exercise to improve your sentence level work.

On your own, with a partner or in a small group; complete the task sheet provided to you by your teacher on page 58.

Once finished, cut off the homework task to take home with you for further practice.

Extension

Write a letter to your teacher explaining why you were late for school. Complete the task on page 59.

Once completed, write your letter and hand it in!

Answers

1 I couldn't leave her on her own; she was petrified!

2 because

3 The lion escaped from the circus; nobody was injured.

Homework

- No specific answers are required for this task, though teachers should check that the examples provided by each learner have included the necessary semi-colon.

Remember...
It is very rare that we use a **semi-colon**. It is half way between a comma and a full stop and acts as a strong pause that links two parts of a sentence.

Semi-colons

You're Late!

"Sorry Miss, I know I'm late but you'll never believe what happened to me on the way to school this morning. Do you know the circus that has come to town?

Well, the lion escaped and caused havoc in the village. Mrs Honeydew was so scared she climbed the cherry tree (you know, the one next to the duck pond) and I had to call the fire brigade to help her down. I couldn't leave her on her own; she was petrified! I wasn't though miss, even when the lion came to have a drink from the duck pond, even when it roared.... er...like a lion, I stood there guarding Mrs Honeydew. I was dead brave Miss, especially when I helped the police put the lion back in its cage. You could ask Mrs Honeydew herself only she packed her bags and flew off to Spain straight after. I think she needed to rest after her ordeal."

Look at the following excuse and answer the questions below.

1 Copy out the sentence in this text that has a semi-colon in it.

1 mark

2 If this semi-colon was replaced with a connective, which one would it most likely be?

and   because   although   also   but   so

2 marks

3 Where would you put the semi-colon in this sentence? Why?

The lion escaped from the circus but nobody was injured.

2 marks

TOP CLASS - Punctuation - Year 3

Semi-colons

You have been asked by your teacher to complete the following exercise to improve your sentence level work. Colour code the two parts of each sentence and copy them out in full below. Don't forget to use a semi-colon to show the big pause.

Sentence level work

	;	
Jason opened the box		Max stood there with muddy paws.
Tom was very clever		Patrick's is in September.
Lee's birthday is in November		two hundred guests are expected.
Alex bought an ipod		she was a nurse and had worked the night shift.
The cat flap swung open		it was empty.
The wedding invitations have been sent		she listened to it as she walked home.
Alisha's mum was tired		he scored top marks in his test.

1. Jason opened the box; it was empty.

2. _____

3. _____

4. _____

5. _____

6. _____

7. _____

Homework
Look through your class reader. Find three examples of a sentence that uses a semi-colon.

Semi-colons

Write a letter to your teacher explaining why you were late for school.
What happened to make you late?
Why was it not your fault?
Why should your teacher believe you?
Why can nobody else back up your story?

Name:

Date:

Punctuation for Parenthesis

Think about...
How might you write a list of instructions?
Why are step by step instructions important?
Why are numbers, letters or Roman numerals often used? What might happen if they weren't used?

Guided

You are reading a recipe for love.

With a partner, make a list of things you might see in this recipe. Think about how it might be set out and what things might be included. What numbers and abbreviations might you see? How will they appear on the page?

Once done, share your ideas with your classmates. Then answer the questions on page 61.

Independent

You want to bake a raspberry marble slice.

On your own, with a partner or in a small group; complete the task sheet provided to you by your teacher on page 62.

Once finished, cut off the homework task to take home with you for further practice.

Extension

Write a set of instructions on how to build a sandcastle. Complete the task on page 63.

Once complete, hold a class competition to see who can build the best one!

Answers

1 1 2 3 4 [5] 6 7 8

2 *Allow for personal response but ensure that their answers begin with 9) and 10) and are in the correct numerical order.

3 We need friends who are (A) kind, (B) loyal and (C) fun.

Homework

- No specific answers are required for this task, though teachers should check that the recipe created by each learner is authentic and that the list of ingredients (or instructions) provided use parenthesis correctly.

Remember...
We use **parenthesis** to separate numbers or letters at the start of a list. When the list is inside a sentence, we use **full parenthesis** in order to enclose the numbers or letters.

Punctuation for Parenthesis

INGREDIENTS FOR LOVE

1) One cup of romance

2) Three tablespoons of trust

3) ½ cup of respect

4) ¾ cup of patience

5 A pinch of humour

6) ¼ lb of sharing

7) A teaspoon of tenderness

8) A generous splash of forgiveness

Look at this list of ingredients and answer the questions below.

1 Which ingredient is missing its punctuation for parenthesis?

| 1 | 2 | 3 | 4 | 5 | 6 | 7 | 8 |

1 mark

2 Write down two more ingredients you might need for love.

_____

_____

2 marks

3 Which of these sentences below is punctuated correctly? Tick one box.

We need friends who are A) kind, B) loyal and C) fun. ☐

We need friends who are (A) kind (B) loyal and (C) fun. ☐

We need friends who are (A) kind, (B) loyal, (C) fun. ☐

1 mark

TOP CLASS - Punctuation - Year 3

Punctuation for Parenthesis

Put this recipe in the right order. Don't forget to add your punctuation for parenthesis. You can choose numbers, letters or Roman numerals.

	Raspberry Marble Slice
	Turn off the oven, open the door and leave the tray bake to cool gradually. For best results, chill for at least 1 hour before slicing.
	After 10 minutes take out and remove the beans and paper, then return to the oven for a further 5 minutes.
	Roll out a 375g pack of ready-rolled short crust pastry on a floured surface. Line a 30cm x 20cm tin with the rolled out pastry.
	Whisk together 500g of mascarpone, 100g of caster sugar, 100g of ground almonds and 2 large eggs until smooth.
	Heat oven to 160°C/gas mark 4.
	Pour everything into the tin and bake for 20-25 minutes until lightly golden.
	Once the tin has been lined, cover the pastry with greaseproof paper. Place baking beans on top and cook for 10 minutes.
	Fold in 250g of fresh raspberries and 100g of white chocolate (roughly chopped) into the mixture.

Homework

You want to write a recipe for friendship and present it as a gift. Write a list of ingredients you will need for this recipe. You may use some of the ideas from the recipe for love to help you. How will you decorate and present this as a gift?

Punctuation for Parenthesis

You are taking a friend to the seaside for the very first time! Write a set of instructions to help them build a sand castle. What equipment will you need? What will you need to do first? What will your next steps be? How will you decorate your castle?

Name: **Date:**

How to Build a Sand Castle

You will need:

About the author of this book

John Murray

John Murray is a recognised specialist in developing children's reading skills through interactive and kinaesthetic approaches.

Since graduating from the University of North Wales in 1997, with a Bachelor of Education degree in English and Communication, John has taught in a wide variety of schools and situations. His experience includes teaching pupils with complex language difficulties and in communities where English is not the first language. Such challenging experiences have inspired John to create innovative new approaches to the teaching and learning of Literacy; developing techniques, ideas and methods that benefit all in the classroom.

Having created the best selling *Reading Explorers* series – highly regarded in schools across Britain and sold worldwide, he balances his teaching with his work as an independent writer and lectures on how to develop key literacy skills in leading colleges and universities. He also provides both internal and external training courses for schools.

For more information regarding resources and training from John Murray visit: **www.johnmurraycpd.co.uk**